R03675

St. Mary's

D0247900

18 APR 2012

OLYMPIC SPORTS

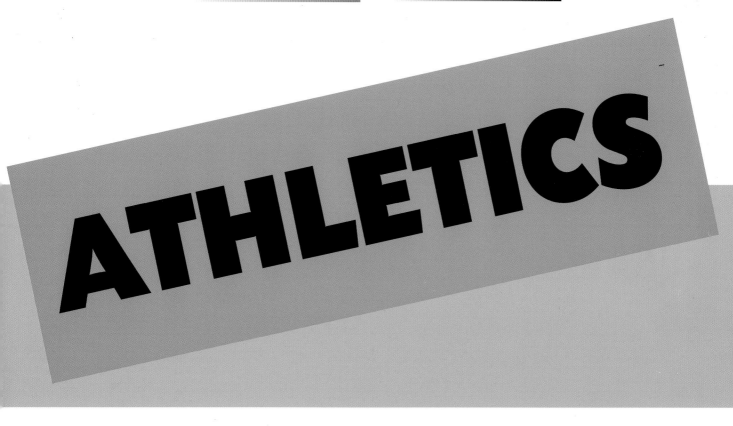

ATHLETICS

Clive Gifford

W
FRANKLIN WATTS
LONDON•SYDNEY

An Appleseed Editions book

Paperback edition 2012

First published in 2011 by Franklin Watts
338 Euston Road, London NW1 3BH

Franklin Watts Australia
Hachette Children's Books
Level 17/207 Kent St, Sydney, NSW 2000

© 2011 Appleseed Editions

Created by Appleseed Editions Ltd,
Well House, Friars Hill, Guestling,
East Sussex TN35 4ET

Designed by Helen James
Edited by Mary-Jane Wilkins
Picture research by Su Alexander

All rights reserved. No part of this publication may be reproduced, stored in a
retrieval system or transmitted in any form or by any means, electronic, mechanical,
photocopying, recording or otherwise, without prior permission of the publisher.

ISBN 978-1-4451-1391-3

Dewey Classification 796.4'2

A CIP catalogue for this book is available from the British Library.

Picture credits
Page 4 Getty Images; 5 AFP/Getty Images; 6 Sports Illustrated/Getty Images;
7 AFP/Getty Images; 8 & 9 Sports Illustrated/Getty Images; 10 Jonathan Larsen/
Shutterstock; 11 AFP/Getty Images; 12 AFP/Getty Images; 13 Pete Niesen/
Shutterstock; 14 & 15 Getty Images; 16 Sports Illustrated/Getty Images; 17 & 18
Getty Images; 19 & 20 AFP/Getty Images; 21 & 22 Getty Images; 23, 24 & 25 AFP/
Getty Images; 26 Getty Images; 27t Muzsy/Shutterstock, b AFP/Getty Images;
28t AFP/Getty Images, b Getty Images; 29t AFP/Getty Images, b Getty Images
Front cover: AFP Getty Images

Printed in Singapore

Franklin Watts is a division of Hachette Children's Books,
an Hachette UK company.
www.hachette.co.uk

Contents

4 Going for gold

6 Sprint races

10 Relay races

12 Hurdles

14 Longer races

16 The marathon

18 Long jump

20 High jump

24 Javelin

26 Other field events

28 Gold medal greats

30 Glossary

31 Books and websites

32 Index

Going for gold

The Olympics is the greatest sporting show on Earth. More than 12,000 athletes (Olympians) flock to one country every four years to compete in their sport during 17 action-packed days. Winning an Olympic gold, silver or bronze medal for finishing first, second or third in an event is a highlight of many athletes' sporting careers.

The US 4 x 400m relay team (from left to right: LaShawn Merritt, Angelo Taylor, David Neville and Jeremy Wariner) with their gold medals at the 2008 Beijing Olympics.

ANCIENT ATHLETICS

The ancient Olympics began in Greece in 776 BCE. At first there was just one sporting event, a race over a distance called a *stade* (around 190 metres) from which the word stadium comes. Over time, events were added. Most were athletics events, such as races run over varying distances or throwing and jumping events including the discus and long jump.

MODERN GAMES

The ancient Olympics were held for more than 1,000 years before they were banned by the Roman emperor Theodosius. He was a

Christian who believed that the games were **pagan**. Then in 1896, the Olympics were revived at the first modern Olympic games held in Athens, Greece. Athletes competed in swimming and other sports, but athletics was centre stage and has remained so ever since. Athletics involves track events – running and **racewalking** – and field events such as jumping, throwing and vaulting competitions.

DECATHLON AND HEPTATHLON

Athletes compete on both track and field in two events. The seven-event **heptathlon** for women and the ten-event **decathlon** for men are both held over two days of intense competition. Each athlete's time in a race, or distance covered in a jump or throw, is converted into points and the winner is the athlete with the most points.

British athlete Jessica Ennis competes in the long jump at the 2010 World Indoor Championships. As a leading heptathlete, Ennis is aiming for a medal at the 2012 Olympics.

Super Star

Most Olympic athletes train for years to take part in the Olympics. The American Bob Mathias began training for the decathlon event just four months before the 1948 Olympics. Amazingly, he won the gold medal. He repeated the feat in 1952.

FEATS AND RECORDS

The first modern Olympic games event was an athletics event – the triple jump. The winner, American James Connolly, had a great games, coming second in the high jump and third in the long jump.

5

Sprint races

Usain Bolt (wearing number 7) drives out of the blocks at the start of the 100 metres Olympic final where he shattered the world record with a time of 9.69 seconds.

The fastest men and women on the planet compete in races over distances which range from 60-metre sprints held indoors to 400 metres or a complete **lap** of the track. To become Olympic champion in the 100 metres is one of sport's greatest prizes.

QUICK OFF THE BLOCKS

Competition is fierce in sprinting and athletes run a number of races called **heats**. Only the fastest eight reach the final. Athletes begin in a crouching position, with their feed on angled supports called **starting blocks**. When the starter pistol fires, they power off their blocks.

FALSE STARTS

Sprinters need a fast start, but if they move too soon the electronic sensors on their starting blocks signal a false start. In the past, a sprinter with two false starts was **disqualified**. In 2010 the starting rules were changed. Now, the first athlete to make a false start is disqualified.

RACE PACE

As they leave their blocks, sprinters drive forward from a low position and gradually straighten up until they are upright and reach their top speed. This can be as fast as 40 km/h. Sprinters concentrate on a smooth and flowing running style and try to maintain their top speed, or pace, right to the finish line. An athlete completes a race when their **trunk** crosses the finish line, rather than their legs or head.

Olympic OoPs

British sprinter Linford Christie won a silver at the 1988 Olympics and gold at the 1992 games, but in the 1996 100 metre final was disqualified after two false starts.

FEATS AND RECORDS

At 16, American Betty Robinson became the first women's athletics gold medallist when she won the 100 metres at the 1928 Olympics. These were the first games to include track and field athletics for women.

PHOTO FINISHES

Some races are amazingly close and officials use high-speed cameras to look at photo finishes and decide on a runner's position. At the 2008 Olympics, Jamaican sprinters Sherone Simpson and Kerron Stewart both finished the 100 metre sprint with the same time of 10.98 seconds and could not be separated into second and third, so they were both awarded silver medals.

Jamaica's Shelly-Ann Fraser (third from right) wins gold in the women's 100 metre sprint at the 2008 Olympics. A total of 85 sprinters took part in the women's 100 metre competition.

Michael Johnson (left) streaks ahead of Roger Black (second left) during the 1996 400 metre final. Johnson set a new Olympic record for the race, finishing in 43.49 seconds. Roger Black won the silver medal.

THE 200 METRE SPRINT

The 200 metre race begins on the bend of the track and ends when the runners cross the finishing line at the end of the **home straight.** Instead of starting in a straight line across the track, 200 metre runners have a staggered start so that they all run the same distance. Runners must stay in their lane and they usually lean a little into the bend. They reach maximum speed when they power out of the bend and run down the straight, but face a battle to keep up that speed all the way to the finish line.

DOUBLING UP

Many sprinters enter both the 100 and 200 metre races at the Olympics. A handful of superb athletes have won both, including the exciting Jamaican runner, Usain Bolt, who also added the 4 x 100 metres relay (see page 10) to his 2008 Olympic successes.

THE 400 METRE SPRINT

Athletes also have a staggered start in this race. The distance between each athlete's starting position is greater because runners race around two complete bends in the track. Top Olympians today run this race as an all-out sprint, running

Super Star

Wilma Rudolph suffered from scarlet fever, whooping cough and polio as a child, which left her left leg twisted and in a brace. Rudolph worked incredibly hard to recover and at the 1960 Olympics won gold medals in the 100 and 200 metres, as well as the relay.

FEATS AND RECORDS

At the 1904 Olympics the 200 metre race had no bend as it was held on a straight course. US athlete Archie Hahn won in a record time of 21.6 seconds. His Olympic record was not broken until 1932.

each 100 metres in little more than 11 seconds. American Michael Johnson's 400m world record stands at just 43.18 seconds.

A DIFFICULT DOUBLE

Not many athletes have won both the 200 and 400 metre races. In 1996, something amazing happened. Both Michael Johnson and Marie-José Pérec of France won their 200 and 400 metre events. Both also set new Olympic record times which have not yet been beaten.

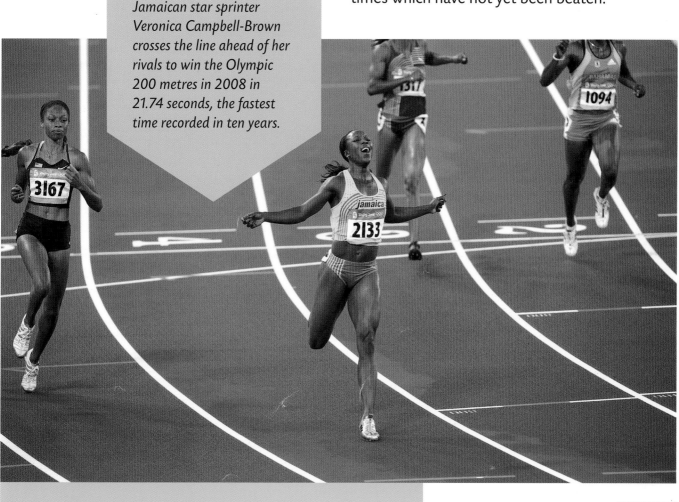

Jamaican star sprinter Veronica Campbell-Brown crosses the line ahead of her rivals to win the Olympic 200 metres in 2008 in 21.74 seconds, the fastest time recorded in ten years.

Relay races

Relay races are team events for four runners. Each runner covers the same distance, running one at a time while carrying a hollow metal tube called a **baton**. The baton is then passed to the next runner in the relay – this is called an exchange or change over.

Runners exchange the baton in the men's 4 x 400m relay at the 2004 Olympics. Teams try to lose as little time as possible during the exchange.

FAST AND FURIOUS

Men ran the 4 x 100 metres relay for the first time at the 1912 Olympics. The first women's race was run in 1928. It is one of the most exciting track races. The four team members each run such a fast lap of the track that the men's world record of 37.10 seconds is more than six seconds faster than the individual 400m world record.

FEATS AND RECORDS
One of the oldest Olympic records still standing was set by the East German women's 100 metre relay team, who won gold in 41.60 seconds in 1980.

CHANGING OVER

The lightning speed of the runners in the 4 x 100 metre relay means that every runner must time their start and baton exchange accurately. The exchange takes place on a 20 metre section of the track called the **changeover** zone. If runners do not exchange the baton within the zone or a runner strays out of the lane, their team is disqualified.

THE 4 X 400 METRE RELAY

The first runner in a 4 x 400 metre race runs a lap in one lane. The runner passes the baton to the second runner, who runs past a line called the **break line** after 100 metres. At this point, all the runners leave their lanes and head to the inside lane, which is the shortest distance round the track. The third **leg** runner and the **anchor** (the final runner) both run on the inside lane.

Olympic OoPs

The US men's and women's 4 x 100 metre teams both entered the 2008 Olympics with strong medal chances. Their hopes faded when both teams dropped the baton and failed to qualify for the final. Jamaica won the men's competition and Russia the women's.

DROPPED!

A runner who drops the baton, in either the 4 x 100 or 4 x 400 metre races, is not disqualified, but recovering the baton loses vital seconds, so the team continues the race a long way behind its competitors.

Runners in the Russian 4 x 100 metre relay team exchange the baton during the 2008 Olympic final. The Russians won, with Belgium second and Nigeria third.

Hurdles

DOHA 2010

Cuba's Dayron Robles won the 2008 Olympics 110m hurdles in 12.93 seconds. He was the only hurdler under 13 seconds in the final.

Hurdles are barriers placed in set positions across the track, which athletes jump over as they race around the track. There are three different hurdling events at the Olympics.

SPRINT HURDLES

Women run sprint hurdle races over 100 metres, and men race over 110 metres. Athletes clear ten hurdles between the start and finish line, using a technique they perfect over years of training. The hurdles fall easily if they are touched. This allows runners to continue racing, but sometimes a runner falls as a result.

THE 400 METRE HURDLES

Men first ran the 400 metre hurdles race at the 1900 Olympics, but women had to wait until 1984 to compete. During the race, athletes clear ten barriers around the track. Each runner stays in one lane, just as in a regular 400 metre race. They need to hit the right **stride pattern** between hurdles, which is hard near the end of a race when their leg muscles tire.

Top hurdlers complete the race in only three or four more seconds than runners in races without hurdles. The US men's hurdlers have a terrific record at the Olympics, and have won 18 of the 24 competitions. In 2008 they scooped all three medals.

The 100m hurdles is often an incredibly close race. The 2008 women's 100m Olympic final was won by US hurdler Dawn Harper.

THE STEEPLECHASE

This exciting event is run over 3,000 metres. Men have competed in the steeplechase since 1896 but the first women's event was held at the 2008 Olympics. Competitors jump 28 large hurdles across the track and clear a water jump seven times during the race. Despite the obstacles, steeplechasers run at high speeds throughout the race. The 2008 women's gold medallist, Russia's Gulnara Galkina-Samitova, broke the world record with a scorching time of 8 minutes, 58.81 seconds.

Olympic OoPs

Finland's Volmari Iso-Hollo won the 1932 Olympic steeplechase in a time of 10:33.4, a minute slower than the time he ran to qualify. This was because an official forgot how many laps had been run and all competitors ran an extra lap.

Super Star

US athlete Edwin Moses is the greatest 400 metre hurdler of all time. Between 1977 and 1987, he ran in 122 races and won them all! This included two Olympic races in which he won gold medals, in 1976 and 1984.

Steeplechasers clear the water jump in the men's 2008 Olympic final. The race was won by Kenya's Brimin Kipruto, who became the seventh Kenyan in a row to win this event.

Longer races

When athletes run longer races, they need huge powers of **endurance**. Their aim is to survive the fast and gruelling pace and to keep enough energy in reserve to sprint for the line at the finish.

Britain's Kelly Holmes raises her arms as she wins her second gold medal of the 2004 games, the 1,500 metres, with Russia's Tatyana Tomashova coming second and Maria Cioncan of Romania third.

MIDDLE DISTANCE RACING

The 800 and 1,500 metres are the middle distance events at an Olympics. Runners complete each lap at high speed and try to save a little energy for a sprint to the line at the end. A number of athletes double up and enter both races but only five (two men and three women) have won both at the same Olympics. The last athlete to do this was Kelly Holmes.

THE 5,000 METRES

This race is a test of speed and **stamina**, as runners increase speed in the last laps. At the Olympics, 15 runners contest the 5,000 metres final, selected from the fastest runners in three heats. The first four finishers in each heat plus the three fastest losers overall enter the final. Until 1996, women ran only 3,000 metres.

Super Star

Emil Zatopek set an incredible 20 long distance running world records during his career. At the 1952 Olympics in Helsinki, he achieved something no long distance runner has ever equalled, winning the 5,000m, 10,000m and marathon gold medals. It was his first marathon!

Olympic OoPs

The 1984 Olympic women's 3,000m was expected to be a contest between US runner Mary Decker and Zola Budd, who ran for Great Britain. Budd, who ran barefoot, was ahead of Decker when their legs became entangled. Decker fell and was out of the race. Budd ran on, but finished seventh.

THE 10,000 METRES

This is the longest track race at the Olympics. Men first ran it in 1912 and women in 1988. Athletes run 25 laps at a fast, even pace. They keep an eye on their rivals, who try to break away into a lead, while saving enough energy to make a dash for the finishing line in the last laps. Athletes run each lap of the track in not much more than a minute.

AMAZING AFRICANS

African runners have won almost all the medals in the men's 5,000 and 10,000 metres at recent Olympics. Only one of the 18 medals awarded for the 10,000 metres in the past six Olympics has gone to a non-African runner. Ethiopia's Kenenisa Bekele holds the record of 27 minutes 5.1 seconds. Tirunesh Dibaba, also from Ethiopia, holds the women's record of 29 minutes 54.66. In 2008, she won both the 5,000 and 10,000 metre Olympic races.

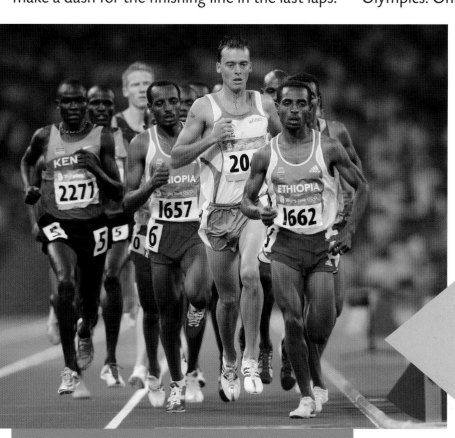

Ethiopia's Tariku Bekele leads the pack as they run down the track straight during the 5,000m final of the 2008 games. Bekele finished sixth and his brother, Kenenisa, won the gold medal.

The marathon

The longest running race of all at an Olympics is the marathon. It is named after the legend of Pheidippides, an ancient Greek messenger who is said to have run from the Battle of Marathon to Athens around 490 BCE.

Kenyan marathon runner Samuel Kamau Wanjiru crosses the line to win the gold medal at the 2008 games. His time was nearly three minutes faster than the previous record.

OLYMPIC COURSES

Since the 1924 games, the marathon course has been 42.195 kilometres long. Each course varies depending on the **terrain** of the city the games are held in. At the 2012 games, the course runs through central London past many famous landmarks before reaching the Olympic stadium. At the end of every Olympic marathon, runners enter the athletics stadium and complete one lap of the track to finish.

Super Star

Abebe Bikila won the 1960 Olympic marathon in bare feet. The Ethiopian athlete competed at the last minute and had no running shoes which fitted well. Bikila won the marathon again in 1964 – this time wearing shoes.

ALONG THE WAY

Running a marathon is a gruelling task. In the men's 2008 marathon, 22 of the 98 competitors who started did not finish the race. There are refreshment stalls alongside the course at five kilometre intervals where runners can grab a sports drink or water while running. Sponging stations also line the route, allowing runners to squeeze a sponge soaked in cold water over their heads and bodies.

PACE AND STAMINA

It's sometimes hard to judge from television images just how fast athletes are running in a marathon. The speeds are astonishing. Top marathon runners cover every kilometre in about three minutes and keep up this rate over the entire race. The 2008 men's winner, Samuel Kamau Wanjiru set a new Olympic record of

2 hours 6 minutes 32 seconds. Constantina Dita of Romania won the women's race in 2 hours 26 minutes 44 seconds and at the age of 38 became the oldest Olympic marathon winner in history.

Olympic OOPs

Early Olympic marathons weren't always carefully checked. American Fred Lorz crossed the line first at the 1904 marathon and was greeted by cheering crowds, only to admit later that he had taken a lift in a car for 17 kilometres of the race. Cheat!

Top runners cross Tower Bridge during the 2010 London Marathon. The race was won for the first time by Russian athlete Liliya Shobukhova.

Long jump

The long jump is one of the most explosive of all field athletics events. Competitors sprint fast down a narrow strip of track called the **runway** and leap as far as they can, landing in a long sandpit.

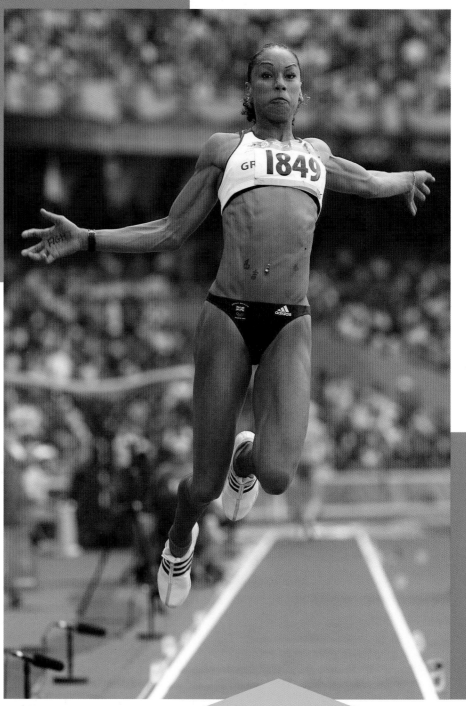

RUN-UPS AND NO JUMPS

Long jumpers pace their run-up very carefully. Their aim is to reach maximum speed before they leap off a panel in front of the sandpit called the take-off board. They must place the foot on or behind the board – if they overstep the board, officials wave a red flag to signal a **no jump**, which doesn't count even if it is very long.

GOOD LANDING

Jumpers aim to stay in the air as long as they can. When they land they collapse their legs into the sand and try to avoid leaning back or placing their hands behind them. This is because each jump is measured from the take-off board to the mark nearest to it that the athlete's body has made in the sand.

Jade Johnson flies through the air during the 2008 Olympic long jump. Johnson's longest jump of 6.64 metres was 40 centimetres shorter than the winning jump of Maurren Higa Maggi.

CHAMPION JUMPERS

The men's long jump has been part of every modern Olympics. US jumpers have won 21 of the 26 competitions held. Women first competed in the long jump at the 1948 Olympics and winners have come from all over the world, including New Zealander Yvette Williams, German Heike Drecshler and Brazilian Maurren Higa Maggi, who became the 2008 champion.

SPRINTING SUCCESS

Top long jumpers need speed on the runway and some leading jumpers are also successful sprint racers. US Olympic legend Jesse Owens won four gold medals in the long jump and sprint races at the 1936 games. The year before, Owens had jumped 8.13m, a world record that lasted 25 years!

Super Star

The most successful of all Olympic long jumpers is American Carl Lewis, who won four Olympic long jump gold medals, as well as a further five Olympic gold medals in sprint races.

FEATS AND RECORDS

Irving Saladino became Panama's first ever Olympic champion in any sport in 2008 when he won the long jump competition with a leap of 8.34 metres. He returned home to a parade of thousands of people.

Panama's Irving Saladino lands after his gold medal-winning long jump of 8.34 metres at the 2008 Olympics. It was his country's first Olympic gold.

High jump

Bryan Clay takes off vertically at the start of a high jump attempt in the men's decathlon. High jumpers aim for a powerful spring up and over the bar.

e high jump is one of the most exciting
tics events. Athletes need rhythm,
ility and explosive jumping power
leap over a bar often set at a
above their heads.

JUMP ST

The high j
on supports
the bar as the tre-long bar which rests
supports for th allowed to touch
jumpers used al must stay on the
1968 American Dnt. In the past,
iques, then in
unned rivals

20

FEATS AND RECORDS

Javier Sotomayor from Cuba set the men's world record in 1993, a year after he had won Olympic gold. His leap of 2.45 metres has never been bettered.

with a head-first technique called the Fosbury flop. This is used by all top athletes today.

THREE ATTEMPTS

Olympic high jumpers usually have three attempts at each height. If they fail to clear the bar after the third attempt they are out of the competition. As jumpers succeed at a height, the bar is raised and every jumper has three attempts at clearing the new height. The competition continues until only one athlete clears a height – the winner!

COUNTBACK

The distances separating high jumpers are often tiny. If more than one athlete clears the winning

Super Star

Iolanda Balas not only won two Olympic gold medals in the women's high jump, she also broke the world record 14 times. Between 1957 and 1967 she won 140 high jump competitions in a row!

height, the winner is the one who made the fewest attempts. This is known as **countback**. At the 2008 games, Blanka Vlasic and Tia Hellebaut both cleared 2.05 metres, but Hellebaut won gold and Vlasic silver as Vlasic needed more attempts to clear that height.

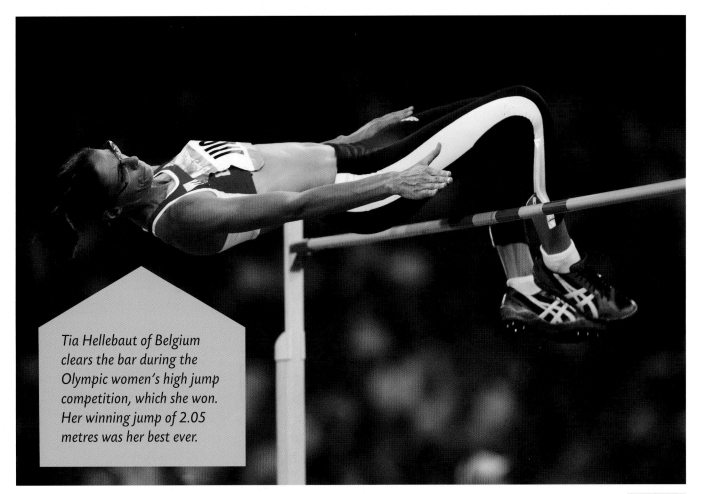

Tia Hellebaut of Belgium clears the bar during the Olympic women's high jump competition, which she won. Her winning jump of 2.05 metres was her best ever.

Discus

Athletes throw the discus using a sweeping arm movement. The first event was held at the ancient Olympics in 708 BCE using a stone and bronze discus. The men's discus competition has been part of every modern Olympics and the women's competition was first held in 1928.

American Stephanie Brown Trafton wins the 2008 Olympic women's discus competition. Her victory was a surprise as throwers from Russia, Germany and Eastern Europe have dominated women's discus at the Olympics.

FEATS AND RECORDS

French athlete Micheline Ostermeyer won the gold medal in the 1948 women's discus event. She also won gold in the shot-put and a bronze in the high jump.

THROWING CIRCLE

A discus thrower starts at the back of a 2.5-metre-wide throwing circle. Throwers enter the circle from the back and use every centimetre of the circle space as they turn round and round, making long rhythmic swings led by the arm holding the discus.

ROUND AND ROUND

Throwers spin round, building speed and power until their bodies face the front of the circle. The arm and hand holding the discus is behind, and whips forward past the rest of the body with enormous power. Then the thrower releases the discus, pressing the fingers on its edge to help it spin away sweetly.

Super Star

Al Oerter became the youngest Olympic discus champion in 1956 at the age of 20. He went on to win four Olympic discus competitions in a row, though he didn't make his longest ever throw of 69.49 metres until 1980.

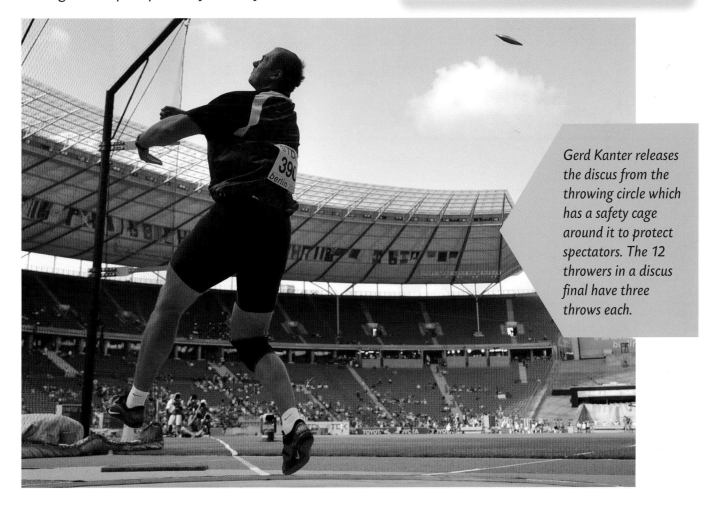

Gerd Kanter releases the discus from the throwing circle which has a safety cage around it to protect spectators. The 12 throwers in a discus final have three throws each.

LONG DISTANCE DISCUS

The discus is one event in which women have thrown longer distances than men. This is partly because a woman's discus weighs one kilo and a men's discus two kilos. With a well-timed, powerful throw, top Olympic athletes can throw the discus well over 60 metres.

WORLD RECORD THROWS

In the men's discus, no one has beaten Jürgen Schult's world record of 74.08 metres. The German set this world record years ago, in 1986. During the 1970s, Faina Melnik broke the women's world record 11 times and won the gold medal at the 1972 Olympics.

Javelin

Javelin throwers need skill and timing, as well as strength, to hurl the javelin over long distances. Top throwers can send the javelin away at speeds of more than 100 km/h.

Norway's Andreas Thorkildsen draws back the javelin just before unleashing it during the men's javelin final at the Beijing games in 2008. Thorkildsen repeated his 2004 gold medal success in Beijing.

THE JAVELIN

In the ancient Olympics, the javelin was a straight branch cut from an olive tree. Until the 1950s, many competitors used a javelin made of bamboo. Today, the javelin is a hollow metal tube around 2.6 metres long for men and 2.2 metres long for women. It has a sharp point at its nose and a cord grip around halfway along its length.

RUNWAY AND TAKE-OFF

Javelin throwers start each throw at the end of a narrow corridor called a runway. They build up speed holding the javelin level with the ground at head height. Turning to face the side, they draw the javelin back, then whip their arm and body forward to unleash it with explosive power. The distances thrown can be enormous.

Olympic OoPs

There was a two-handed javelin competition at the 1912 Olympics. Finland won all three medals in the men's event, in which an athlete's best throw with the left and right hand were added together.

Mariya Abakumova of Russia releases the javelin during an Olympic competition. Her powerful follow-through and angle of release gave her a throw of over 70 metres, enough to win the silver medal.

At the 2008 games, Norway's Andreas Thorkildsen won gold with a throw of 90.57 metres, the longest ever at an Olympics.

A WINNING THROW

A winning throw has to be long, but also straight so that it lands in the throwing sector. Throwers try to release the javelin at an angle so that it lands nose first, otherwise officials signal a **no throw**. In the Olympics final, competitors are allowed three throws and the top eight athletes then have a further three throws each.

Super Star

Jan Zelezny from the Czech Republic won silver in the 1988 Olympics and went on to greater success during the 1990s. He won three gold medals in a row at the 1992, 1996 and 2000 Olympics. His 1996 world record throw was a whopper – 98.48 metres.

Other field events

A number of other field athletics events are held at the Olympics and at other major international athletics competitions.

US shot-putter Reese Hoffa cradles the shot beside his neck before leaning back and then driving forward explosively to put the shot. Shot-putters dust their hands with chalk for a good grip.

SHOT-PUT

The shot is a solid metal ball weighing 7.26 kilos for men and 4 kilos for women. Shot-putters cradle the ball in one hand while standing in a small throwing circle, then swivel round, throwing the arm up and outwards to launch the shot into the air. The 2008 Olympic champions – Tomasz Majewski of Poland and Valerie Vili of New Zealand – regularly throw the shot more than 20 metres.

Olympic OoPs

While practising shortly before the shot-put final, Randy Barnes was hit in the back by a put from US teammate John Godina. The accident didn't stop Barnes winning gold with a throw of 21.62 metres. Godina won silver.

A hammer thrower builds speed and momentum in the circle by turning and swinging the hammer.

THE HAMMER

The hammer is a shot-put on a chain almost a metre long attached to a handle. The thrower swings the hammer round, building up speed and power before stepping across the circle and releasing it. The hammer can soar long distances. Aksana Miankova of Belarus won the 2008 women's hammer with a throw of 76.34 metres.

TRIPLE JUMP

Triple jumps are performed on the same runway and pit as the long jump. Athletes try to jump as far as possible. Triple jumpers build up speed before their jump with a hop – leaping off one foot then landing on it. They then make a long step, landing on the opposite foot, before jumping into the pit like a long jumper. The distances covered in this set of moves are amazing – Kenny Harrison set the Olympic record in 1996 with a jump of 18.09 metres.

POLE VAULT

Pole vaulters sprint down a runway and plant one end of their pole in a small slot to vault upwards. The pole bends and then unbends, carrying the vaulter up around 5 metres for women and 6 metres for men. The aim is to clear a bar without knocking it off the supports.

FEATS AND RECORDS

The 1896 Olympic pole vault competition was won by Welles Hoyt with a jump of 3.30 metres. At the 1988 Olympics, Sergey Bubka set a new Olympic record of 5.90 metres – a metre higher than a double decker bus!

Steven Hooker clears the bar after releasing his pole. The Australian athlete won the 2008 Olympics gold with a vault of 5.96 metres.

Gold medal greats

Many competitors train hard and make sacrifices to perform at their best at an Olympics. Competition is fierce in all sports, so only the most talented make it. Here are the stories of four great Olympic athletes.

USAIN BOLT

Nicknamed 'Lightning' for good reasons, the Jamaican runner was disappointed when he didn't progress past the heat of his first Olympics in 2004. Bolt bounced back in sensational style at the 2008 Olympics, where he won the 100 metres, 200 metres and 4 x 100 metre relay, all in astonishing world record times. His run of 9.69 seconds in the 100 metres could have been even faster, but he slowed down in the last 30 metres. Bolt beat both his 100 and 200 metre world records at the 2009 World Championships.

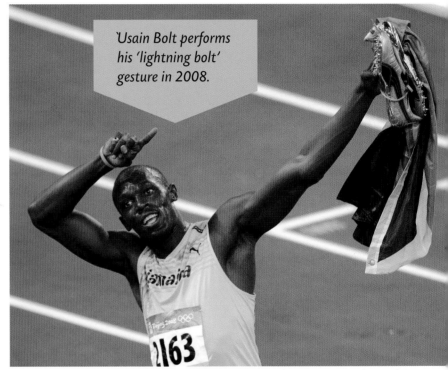

'Usain Bolt performs his 'lightning bolt' gesture in 2008.

FANNY BLANKERS-KOEN

The 1940 and 1944 Olympics were cancelled because of the Second World War. So Dutchwoman Fanny Blankers-Koen first competed at the 1948 games. Women could only enter three individual events at these Olympics. She entered the 100 metres, 80 metre hurdles and 200 metres and won them all. She won her fourth gold of the games in the 4 x 100 metres relay and might have won a fifth and sixth gold medal if she had been allowed to enter the long jump and high jump. Blankers-Koen was the outstanding performer at the 1948 Olympics, and was named female athlete of the century in 1999 by the IAAF, the organization that runs world athletics.

FEATS AND RECORDS
Fanny Blankers-Koen won her 58th and final Dutch national athletics title in 1955. It wasn't in the long jump or a sprint race – it was in the shot-put!

YELENA ISINBAYEVA

Isinbayeva was originally a Russian gymnast who has been a star performer in the women's pole vault since 2003, when she broke the world record by clearing 4.84 metres. She won Olympic gold in 2004 and repeatedly broke the world record. At the 2008 Olympics she set an amazing new high of 5.05 metres to win her second gold medal.

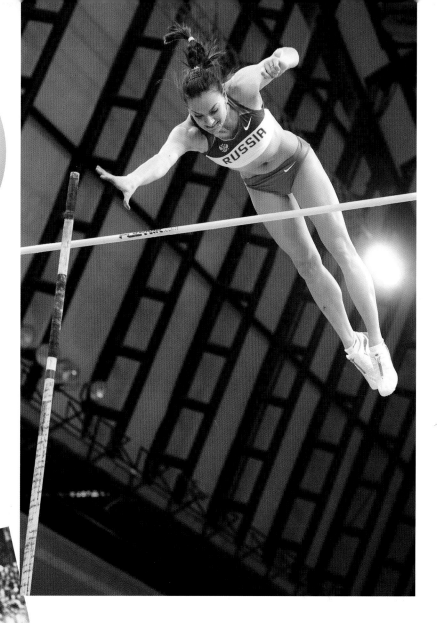

PAAVO NURMI

Paavo Nurmi is Finland's long distance running star. He won a staggering nine Olympic gold medals in a range of races from 1,500 to 10,000 metres at three Olympics (1920, 1924 and 1928). He won five of the medals in just six days during the 1924 games – an astonishing feat. Nurmi also won three silver medals, including one in the 3,000 metre steeplechase in 1928, an event he had run only three times before.

The great Paavo Nurmi crosses the line to win a race in London.

Glossary

anchor   An athlete who runs the last leg in a relay race.

baton   A short, hollow tube carried and passed on by runners in a relay race.

break line   A curved line on the track which shows when runners in a middle distance race can change lane.

changeover   The action of handing the baton from one runner to another in a relay race.

countback   Counting the number of previous failed attempts in a high jump or pole vault competition to determine the winner.

decathlon   An event for men, who compete in ten different track and field events.

disqualify   To remove an athlete from a race or competition for breaking a rule or making a false start in a race.

endurance   The ability to continue competing over a long period of time.

flexibility   The ability of an athlete's joints to move through a full range of motion.

heat   An early race in an athletics competition in which the top athletes go through to the next round.

heptathlon   An event for women, who compete in seven different track and field events.

home straight   The final straight piece of track before the finish line.

lap   A complete circuit of the 400 metre long track.

leg   The section of a relay race run by one athlete.

no jump   An attempt at a jump which is ruled as not counting by officials.

no throw   An attempt at a throw which officials decide has broken the event's rules and so does not count in the competition.

pagan   Not Christian. A pagan has spiritual beliefs which are different from the main world religions and which may involve the worship of nature.

racewalking   Events during which athletes walk very fast around a track or a road course.

runway   The narrow strip which a pole vaulter, long and triple jumper and javelin thrower runs along to build up speed.

stamina   The ability to perform hard physical exercise for long periods of time.

starting blocks   A pair of angled supports on the track from which a sprinter pushes off when starting a race.

stride pattern   The planned number of steps a hurdler takes between hurdles in order to take off correctly and clear a hurdle.

terrain　The type of ground surface that makes up a marathon route or course.

trunk　Your body from your shoulders down to your waist, not including your arms.

Books

Know Your Sport: Field Athletics – Clive Gifford, Watts, 2008
A step-by-step guide to performing a range of field athletics events.

Training To Succeed: Track Athletics – Rita Storey, Watts, 2009
Looks at the lives of young athletes training to become top track athletes, their goals and the challenges they face.

Websites

http://www.olympic.org/en/content/Sports/All-Sports/Athletics/Field/
Olympic web pages about field athletics.

http://www.iaaf.org/
The IAAF is the organization which runs world athletics. Its website has profiles of leading athletes, news and an up-to-date list of world records.

http://www.timesonline.co.uk/tol/sport/more_sport/athletics/article3099603.ece
A list by journalist David Powell of 50 memorable Olympic performances.

http://www.sporting-heroes.net/athletics-heroes/default.asp
Biographies of top athletes which you can search by name, Olympic performance and country.

http://news.bbc.co.uk/sport1/hi/athletics/default.stm
The BBC's athletics web pages include the latest news from competitions and information on events and top performers.

http://www.track-and-field.net/
A superb collection of links to websites split into categories, including athletes' personal websites and sites about individual athletics events.

Index

anchor 11, 30

baton 10, 11, 30
Blankers-Koen, Fanny 28, 29
Bolt, Usain 6, 8, 28
break line 11, 30

changeover zone 11, 30
countback 21, 30

decathlon 5, 20, 30
discus 4, 22-23
disqualification 6, 7, 11, 18, 25, 30

endurance 14, 30
exchange 10, 11

false starts 6, 7
flexibility 20, 30

hammer 27
heptathlon 5, 30
high jump 5, 20-21, 22
hurdles 12-13, 28

Isinbayeva, Yelena 29

javelin 24-25

long jump 4, 5, 18-19, 27

marathon 16-17

Nurmi, Paavo 29

pole vault 27, 29

racewalking 5, 30
relay races 10-11
runway 18, 24, 27, 30

shot-put 22, 26, 27, 29
sprint races 6-9, 19
stamina 14, 17, 30
starting blocks 6, 7, 30
steeplechase 13, 29
stride pattern 12, 30
swimming 5

take-off board 18
terrain 16, 31
throwing circle 22, 23, 26, 27
training 5, 12, 28
triple jump 5, 27